NATIVE NATIONS OF
CALIFORNIA

BY THERESE NABER

The Child's World®

Published by The Child's World®
1980 Lookout Drive • Mankato, MN 56003-1705
800-599-READ • www.childsworld.com
Acknowledgments
The Child's World®: Mary Berendes, Publishing Director
Red Line Editorial: Editorial direction and production
The Design Lab: Design
Content Consultant: Dr. Deirdre A. Almeida, Edward C. Johnson
Endowed Director of American Indian Studies Program, Eastern
Washington University American Indian Education Center

Photographs ©: Tomas Ovalle/The Fresno Bee/AP Images,
cover, 2; Paul Marcus/Shutterstock Images, 1, 18; Damian
Dovarganes/AP Images, 3 (top), 3 (middle top), 32, 35; Jeff
Barnard/AP Images, 3 (middle bottom), 12, 14; Darin Barry CC
2.0, 3 (bottom), 7, 26; Robert Bohrer/Shutterstock Images, 5,
39; Michael Fraley CC 2.0, 6; Ed Kashi/VII/Corbis, 8; Edward S.
Curtis/Library of Congress, 9; Marilyn Angel Wynn/Nativestock
Pictures/Corbis, 10, 17; U.S. Forest Service, 13; Kent Porter, Santa
Rosa Press Democrat/AP Images, 16; iStock/Thinkstock, 20; U.S.
Department of Agriculture, 22-23; Ted Soqui/Corbis, 24; Kippy
Spilker/Shutterstock Images, 25; Eric Paul Zamora/Fresno Bee/
AP Images, 27; David McNew/Getty Images News/Thinkstock,
28; National Park Service, 29; Nik Wheeler/Corbis, 30; Lance
Cheung/U.S. Department of Agriculture, 34; Charlie Neuman/
U-T San Diego/ZumaPress/Alamy, 36

Copyright © 2016 by The Child's World®
All rights reserved. No part of this book may be
reproduced or utilized in any form or by any means
without written permission from the publisher.
ISBN: 9781634070294
LCCN: 2014959725
Printed in the United States of America
Mankato, MN
July, 2015
PA02269

ABOUT THE AUTHOR

Therese Naber is a writer who lives in Minnesota. She has coauthored more than ten textbooks and workbooks for students and teachers of English as a second language. She has also written many tests and online activities for language learning.

A memb
Nation
Californ
Day Co
in 2002

TABLE OF CONTENTS

ARCTIC

OCEAN

GREENLAND

Gulf of
Alaska

PACIFIC

OCEAN

Hudson
Bay

CANADA

ATLANTI

OCEAN

UNITED STATES

CALIFORNIA
NATIVE NATIONS

N
W   E
S

MEXICO

Gulf of
Mexico

CHAPTER ONE

CALIFORNIA NATIVE NATIONS

The state of California has amazing geographic diversity. There are mountain ranges, deserts, valleys, lakes, and rivers. The Pacific Ocean runs along California's western edge. It forms 840 miles (1,350 km) of coastline. Between the Coastal Mountains

California's Pacific Coast provides abundant resources from sea and land.

Re-created Yurok village, Patrick's Point State Park, California

and the Sierra Nevada lies the Central Valley. Major rivers flow through the area. The Central Valley contains much of the state's important farmland. The climate of California also varies. Sunshine, warm temperatures, and dry conditions are typical in southern parts of the state. Northern areas of the state tend to be cooler and wetter.

The diversity of landscape and climate shows in the differences in culture, languages, and traditions of the region's Native Nations. But there are also similarities. Native Peoples have lived in what is now California for thousands of years. More than 300,000 people likely lived in the region before Europeans came. They represented more than 500 groups. Most early California Native Peoples were hunter-gatherers. They lived on the abundant wild plant foods and game in the region.

Populations grew and prospered in California for a long time. But Europeans came to establish **missions** and acquire land in the late 1700s. This brought dramatic changes. Missions worked to get Native Peoples to accept the Christian religion. Some accepted but many did not. Many people were forced to live and work in the missions. The contact with nonnatives also brought new diseases. Countless Native People died. After the United States took possession of the region, many more Native People were forced off their land, died, or were killed. The population in the region fell by more than 90 percent in two generations. But the people and their cultures continue.

In 2015 in California, there are more than 100 tribes recognized by the U.S. government. Three are recognized by the

Drum making at the Tule River Indian Reservation is one way residents continue cultural traditions.

state of California only. Many members now live in cities and urban areas. But many others live on **reservations**, or **rancherias**, as they are often known in California. There, they have their own schools, courts, and police forces. The groups have worked hard to maintain their cultural traditions and, in some cases, languages.

Basket weaving is an important traditional Native art in California. Collectors value the baskets. Some can sell for thousands of dollars. However, this art form has been threatened. It became difficult for artists to get the plants they needed for weaving. Plant populations declined, and private owners prevented artists from picking plants on their land. In 1992, California Native Peoples formed the California Indian Basketweavers Association (CIBA) to support the tradition. As a result of CIBA, the number of basketweavers has increased. Today this art form is more secure.

CHAPTER TWO

HUPA

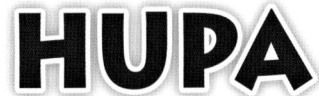

The Hupa people live in the Hoopa Valley. It is in the far northwestern corner of California. There are approximately 2,500 people living on their 85,000-acre (34,000 ha) reservation. They have lived on the same land for thousands of years.

The Hupa people balance logging and conservation in their forest.

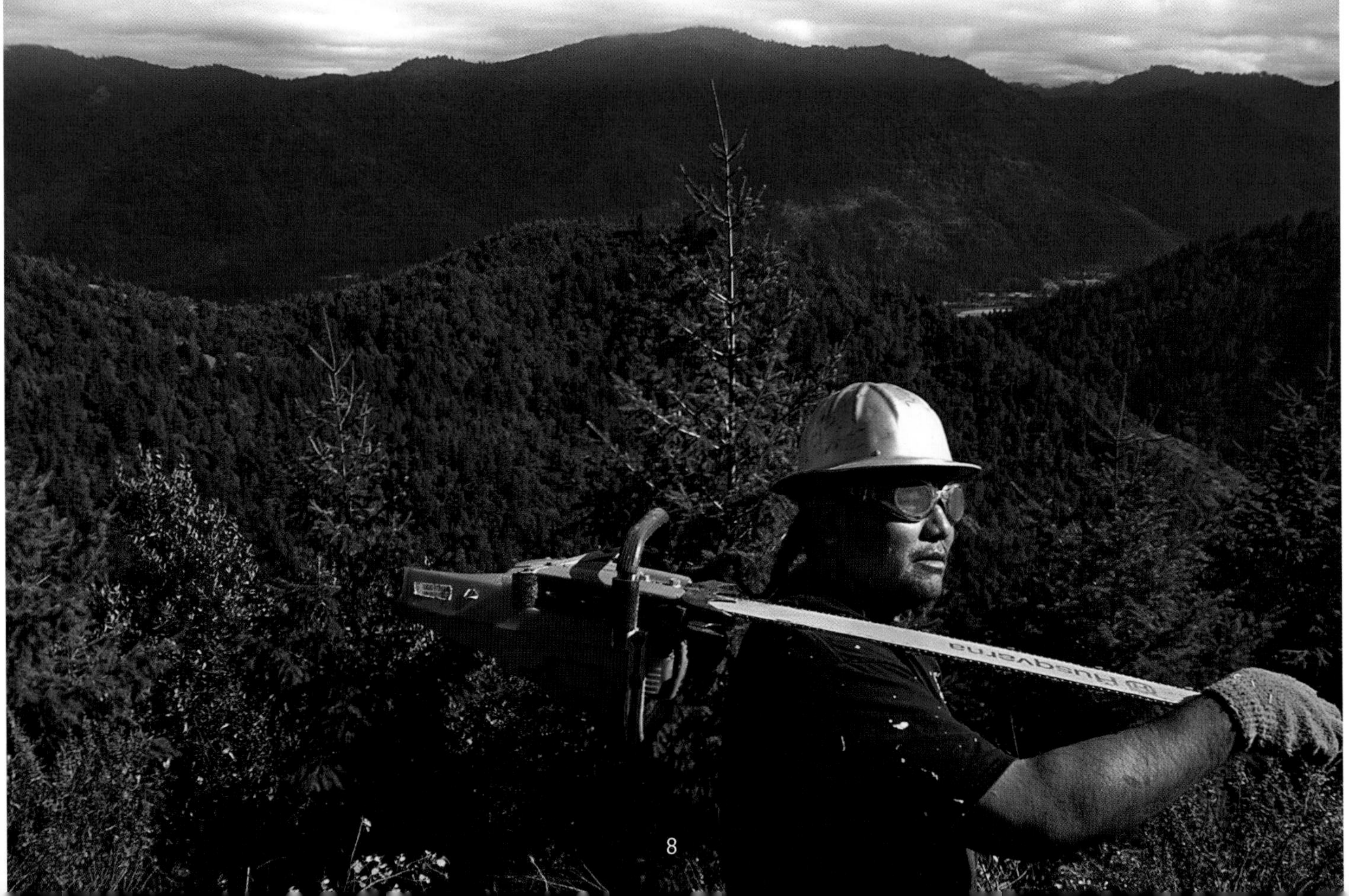

The Hupa have always fished the waters of the Trinity River.

This is unlike many other Native groups, who have been forced to move by nonnative settlers. This has helped the Hupa maintain their culture and traditions. The Hupa language is part of the Athabascan family of languages. The Hupa call themselves *Natinixwe*, which means "People of the Place Where the Trails Return."

Flowing through the reservation is the Trinity River. The river is central to the Hupa's way of life. It provides fish, especially salmon, to the community. Timber from

A woman makes a basket using traditional Hupa methods and materials.

the forest on the reservation is important for residents, too.

The Hupa manage and protect these resources for today and for future generations. The tribal fisheries department reports on fish for the whole river basin. The tribal forestry department manages the forest and monitors wildlife on the reservation. Wildlife found in this area includes black bear, bobcats, bald eagles, and the northern spotted owl. The northern spotted owl is a threatened species, so Hupa researchers monitor it carefully.

Hupa artists are an important part of the Northern California community of artists. Hupa artists make everything from baskets to traditional **regalia** to contemporary jewelry.

Artist George Blake was born on the Hoopa Valley reservation. He studied fine art and Native American art at the University of California, Davis. Blake is known for studying traditional art forms. He taught himself some of these forms. For example, he taught himself how to carve antlers into purses and spoons. He also studied with tribal elders. Now, Blake makes regalia for ceremonial dances. He teaches art and crafts to young people. He is also a successful contemporary artist. He often uses humor in his work to fight stereotypes about Native Peoples.

CHAPTER THREE

YUROK

A Yurok elder makes a canoe for a boat dance that is part of a ceremony for renewing the world.

The Yurok Tribe is the largest tribe in California. It has more than 5,000 members. Most live on the Yurok Reservation. It lies on the lower Klamath River near the Pacific Ocean. The Yurok people have always caught fish in the river—especially salmon—and seafood from the ocean. Historically, canoes were the main way to travel. They were made from fallen redwood trees. The canoe is an important part of Yurok culture, and it is used in traditional religious ceremonies. For example, the White Deerskin Dance gives thanks for what nature has provided. The ceremony uses canoes to transport dancers.

The dance is one of several traditional ceremonies that have been brought back in recent times. As with many other Native communities, Yurok culture and traditions were almost lost. Beginning in the mid to late 1800s, Native children were forced to attend boarding schools. They were sent away from their families. Children in the schools usually were not allowed to speak their culture's language. They could not follow their cultural or religious traditions. As a result, many traditions were no longer passed from generation to generation.

A man shows a traditional Yurok method for cooking fish.

A Yurok wildlife expert examines a turkey vulture. Turkey vultures live in habitats similar to California condors, so the Yurok studied turkey vultures to help develop their plan to bring back condors.

The California condor is one of the largest flying birds in the world. Its average wingspan is almost 10 feet (3 m). The bird is sacred to the Yurok people. It is called *prey-go-neesh* in Yurok. The condor is an important part of some religious ceremonies. Condors used to fly all over California. However, populations dropped due to habitat loss and pollution, and they became endangered. The Yurok Tribe Wildlife Program worked for five years to study condor habitat. Researchers developed a plan to bring the California condor back to their region. The Yurok signed an agreement in 2014 that will allow them to release condors into their area.

The Yurok language is from the same family as the Algonquian language. Many Native Nations in eastern North America speak languages from the Algonquian family. But there are only two groups in California who do. The language almost died out in the 1990s because so few people spoke it. At one point, there were only six speakers. However, tribal leaders were determined not to let it die. They developed a plan to bring back the language. Now, the language is taught in some elementary and high schools in California. It is believed to be the most widely taught Native language in California today.

SAY IT

crow	k'rr'	(kerr)
boat	'yoch	(yuch)
groundhog	wehlkem	(well-kem)
mountain ridge	kerrcherh	(ker-cher)
well/good	kwelekw	(kway-lek)

CHAPTER FOUR

POMO

A Pomo dancer helps dedicate new lands added to the California Coastal National Monument.

The Pomo people live north of the San Francisco Bay. They do not come from one tribe. Instead, the Pomo come from seven different groups that were culturally similar. They spoke seven different languages and could not understand each other.

The Hopland Band of Pomo Indians runs a casino, which brings money to the band.

The Pomo groups were forced off their lands more than once before the beginning of the 20th century. As different groups of nonnative settlers came, they wanted California's rich and productive land. Very often, the Native groups were forced to move, and many died. Around the 1920s, the federal government granted reservation lands called

Basket in the Pomo style

rancherias to the groups. But in 1958, a new law ended the rancherias across California. The lands were broken up for individuals to own rather than the tribes. Losing their land would make the tribes break up, too. But the tribes fought back. Many regained their lands and official recognition through lawsuits. At the beginning of the 21st century, there

Julia Parker is a master basketweaver of Pomo and Miwok descent. Born in 1929, she has worked in Yosemite National Park for many years. She demonstrates her basketry techniques to park visitors. Parker was concerned that these ancient traditions might die out. She has dedicated her life to passing on basket-weaving skills. Samples of her work are in the Smithsonian Institution and in the Queen of England's collection.

were approximately 5,000 members of close to 20 federally recognized Pomo tribes or groups. They live on rancherias in Sonoma, Mendocino, and Lake Counties.

When Nations or tribes are federally recognized, the government considers them **sovereign** nations. They can create their own governments and make their own laws. They also receive benefits and services from the U.S. government. This includes money for education. The federal government also protects their land. Tribes that are not federally recognized do not receive those benefits. Tribes that the state of California recognizes receive state funding.

The traditional arts of the Pomo are based on their natural resources. They make jewelry from clamshells and **abalone**. Pomo baskets are valued throughout the world. They are made from grass and roots.

CHAPTER FIVE

PIT RIVER

Members of the Pit River Tribe live in the northeast of California. Towering Mount Shasta and Lassen Peak mark the region's northwest and southwest corners. The Warner Mountains are the eastern boundary. Twenty peaks taller than 6,000 feet

Mount Shasta rises above the surrounding landscape in northeast California.

The Pit River Band is one member of the Susanville Indian Rancheria. In 2009, the rancheria formed a new tribal business organization called the Susanville Indian Rancheria Corporation (SIRCO). SIRCO supports economic development and the overall well being of tribal members. One of the business's goals is to develop local projects in the Susanville area.

(1,800 m) dot the region. The changes in elevation mean the area has varied climate and vegetation at different heights. The area has a range of food and natural resources. Historically, different Pit River groups ate different foods, used different medicines, and had different materials to make things with, depending on where in the region they lived.

The Pit River Tribe is not just one tribe or nation. Eleven independent bands make up the Pit River people. Bands include the Ajumawi, the Atsugewi, and the Kosalektawi.

They spoke two different languages that were closely related. The population was approximately 1,800 at the beginning of the 21st century. Members live on 12 rancherias. The largest is the XL Ranch. It has more than 9,000 acres (3,600 ha).

The Redding Rancheria is near the town of Redding. The documentary *With the Strength of Our Ancestors* shows the history of this rancheria. It tells the story of dealings between the U.S. government and Native communities from the 1930s onward. For example, in the 1950s and 1960s, the government ended several tribes' federal recognition. As a result, the groups, including the people of the Redding Rancheria, stopped receiving benefits from the government. The Redding Rancheria won its legal battle to become federally recognized again in the

1980s. The history of the rancheria has been full of hardship, and the documentary shows the determination of a people to maintain their cultural and community identity.

The Round Valley Indian Tribe's annual walk commemorates one of the forced relocations California Native Nations endured in the 19th century. The Round Valley group formed when members from several different groups including Pit River were forced to share a reservation. Today the community is unified by its shared history.

CHAPTER SIX

MIWOK

Miwok employees teach visitors about their traditional ways of life at Yosemite National Park.

The Miwok People (also spelled Miwuk, Mi-wuk, or Me-wuk) live in the north-central part of California. Traditionally, the many Miwok bands are divided into four subgroups: Coast Miwok, Plains and Sierra Miwok, Lake Miwok, and Bay

Re-creation of a Miwok roundhouse used for ceremonies

practice traditional religious and cultural ceremonies and create art including baskets. Many of the groups run programs to preserve and support their community. For example, the United Auburn Indian Community (UAIC), made up of Miwok and Maidu members, started the UAIC Community Giving Program in 2004. The program gives money to organizations that help people in the local community. In 2013, the program gave $270,000 to organizations in the community.

Miwok. Many live in their traditional territory today. Some groups are federally recognized, but some are not. The Coast Miwok were recognized as the Graton Rancheria (with Southern Pomo) in 2000. Having official status allows them to receive money for health care, education, and housing.

Today, different Miwok groups are working to bring back their language. They

For more than 34 years, the annual Big Time Festival has been held at Kule Loklo in Point Reyes National Seashore. Kule Loklo is a model of a Coast Miwok village. The Big Time Festival celebrates traditional customs and festivals. There are demonstrations of basketry, bead making, and traditional dancing. The festival is a family event that is free and open to the public.

CHAPTER SEVEN

YOKUTS

Yokuts and Miwok tribal members build a sweat lodge.

Historically, at least 60 tribes or groups made up the Yokuts of central California. They lived in the San Joaquin Valley and up into the foothills of the Sierra Nevada. Most Yokuts prefer to be called by their specific tribal names. Tribes today include the Choinumni, the Chukchansi, the Tache (or Tachi), and the Wukchumni.

The story of the Tache-Yokut Tribe is similar to that of many other tribes. The tribe lives on the Santa Rosa Rancheria, which was established in 1934. By the early 1980s, access to education had increased, but many members lived in poverty. In 1988, the federal government passed the Indian Gaming Regulatory Act (IGRA). This law lets Native Peoples operate casinos on their

The Santa Rosa Rancheria Tachi-Yokut Tribe opened their casino in 2000.

Marie Wilcox is the last **fluent** speaker of the Wukchumni language. The Wukchumni Tribe is part of the Yokuts tribal group. In 2014, there were fewer than 200 members. Wilcox was born in 1933. She spent seven years creating a dictionary of the Wukchumni language. She has also recorded an oral version. It will help learners in the future speak the language.

reservations. The IGRA has been a way for many Native Nations and tribes to rebuild their economies. This has been true for the Tache-Yokut Tribe. They run the Tachi Palace Hotel and Casino. It has had a tremendous impact on the reservation. Unemployment has dropped. The Tache-Yokut see their casino as a way to rebuild their reservation. They hope it will make their economy more self-sufficient. This could help reestablish their cultural identity.

CHAPTER EIGHT

CHUMASH

Cave paintings left by Chumash ancestors, now part of Carrizo Plain National Monument

Historically, the Chumash lived in Southern California around the current Los Angeles area and north to Santa Barbara. Before the Spanish came in the 1500s, the Chumash were one of the largest Native groups in California. They were the

Chumash singers, Santa Monica Mountains National Recreation Area

only tribe in California that got most of its food from ocean fishing. Today, the Chumash continue to be known as great canoe builders.

The Chumash made colorful and detailed paintings on rocks. People who study them believe they were made for religious reasons.

Nineteenth-century Chumash baskets, Santa Barbara Historical Museum

Estimates suggest that most of the paintings are 1,000 years old or less. The paintings show simple human figures and animals as well as abstract designs. They are sacred to the Chumash people. There are many sites with rock paintings. However, the paintings are very delicate and easily damaged. Because it is important to preserve this art, the state

The Chumash once built canoes called *tomols* to travel on the ocean. The canoes were made from redwood trees and were up to 30 feet (9 m) long. Recently, the Chumash have started a *tomol* crossing to celebrate their culture and heritage. Using the traditional boat, paddlers cross the Santa Barbara Channel. It is a 21-mile (34 km) journey.

does not make the location of the paintings public. However, visitors can see rock paintings at the Chumash Painted Cave State Historic Park near Santa Barbara and in some other parks.

Similar to many other Native Peoples in California, the Chumash were badly affected by the missions. Five missions were built in Chumash territory. The Native population went down dramatically. One of the main causes of death was illness from new European diseases.

The Santa Ynez Band of Chumash Indians is the only federally recognized band of the Chumash. There are other groups hoping to get federal recognition in the future. The Santa Ynez Band owns Chumash Casino Resort. The band offers cultural enrichment programs using income from the casino. The programs include language classes, an annual intertribal **powwow**, and Chumash Culture Days, with singing, dancing, and storytelling. The band also created a foundation in 2005 to improve their community.

SAY IT

hello	haku	(ha-ku)
father	kok'o	(kok-o)
mother	xo'ni	(ho-ni)
earth	šup	(shup)
whale	paxat	(pa-jat)

CHAPTER NINE

CAHUILLA

The Cahuilla people live on nine reservations in Southern California. Traditionally, they lived in inland areas of Southern California, mainly south of the San Bernardino Mountains. They were divided into smaller groups. But they all spoke

Members of the Agua Caliente Band of Cahuilla Indians celebrate the dedication of the Santa Rosa and San Jacinto Mountains National Monument with members of the government. The monument includes traditional Cahuilla land.

the same language. Only a few elders speak the language today, and it is endangered.

One group is the Morongo Band of Mission Indians. More than 900 members live on the Morongo Reservation. In 1983, the band started a small bingo hall. Over time, this has developed into a resort, casino, and spa. It is one of the largest tribal gaming facilities in the country.

Bird songs are traditional social songs that tell the history of some Native Peoples. They also give instruction about how to live. They are called "bird songs" because the songs are often told from the viewpoint of birds. They are an important part of culture for Native Nations and tribes in Southern California. The songs are passed from generation to generation. They are used on many occasions, especially when one nation visits another.

The Agua Caliente Band of Cahuilla Indians has a reservation of 32,000 acres (13,000 ha). More than 6,700 of those acres (2,700 ha) are within the city of Palm Springs. It is the city's largest landowner. The group owns casinos, spas, and golf courses in the area. The Agua Caliente Band uses resources from these businesses to support its community. It works with neighboring governments and organizations to improve the whole region. The Agua Caliente Cultural Museum's programs and exhibits share tribal culture with visitors.

CHAPTER TEN

LUISEÑO

Representatives of many nations including the Luiseño form the Council for Native American Farming and Ranching. They work with the U.S. Department of Agriculture to improve farming opportunities for Native People.

Luiseño people live on several reservations and in cities in Southern California. They traditionally lived along the coastline of Southern California and in the San Luis Rey River area. The Spanish named the people after the Mission San Luis

The San Luis Rey Mission hosts an annual intertribal powwow.

Rey de Francia and the river. They are also called the Luiseño Band of Mission Indians. Luiseño farming techniques have always been sophisticated. Ancient farmers used controlled burning to make fields fertile. They managed the water and kept the soil healthy. Today, some continue age-old Luiseño farming methods.

The Luiseño also practice and preserve cultural traditions, such as hunting and gathering, basketry, and rattle making. Unlike some other Native groups, the

This Luiseño gourd rattle has images of sea turtles.

Luiseño people never used drums. Instead, they use rattles to accompany their songs and dances. There are different rattle types. For example, there are deer hoof rattles, turtle shell rattles, and cocoon rattles. Each of these has a specific purpose. The deer hoof rattle represents the sacrifice of the deer. It was the first animal eaten by man, according to

Luiseño **oral histories**. The turtle shell rattle honors the turtle's ability to travel between the worlds of water and air. The cocoon rattle is made from the cocoon of a silk moth. It is a sacred rattle used for private ceremonies. It is not used in public. Most rattles are handed down through families. There are specific rules for caring for a rattle.

The Pechanga Band of Luiseño Mission Indians is one of the larger groups in California today. There are more than 1,300 members. Some live on the Pechanga Reservation near Temecula, California. In

The Pechanga honor their land and natural resources. A great symbol of pride for them is the Great Oak. This huge tree is approximately 20 feet (6 m) around and stands 96 feet (29 m) tall. It is 850 to 1,500 years old—one of the oldest oak trees in the world. In 2002, the land where the tree stands was put into trust. This means the tree is now under Pechanga protection. It will be a symbol of the Pechanga's heritage for generations to come.

the Luiseño language, *Pechanga* means "Place Where the Water Drips." The new Pechanga Cultural Center honors and preserves the band's heritage.

hello!	mííyu	(mee-yoo)
cottonwood tree	avaxat	(a-va-ha)
sycamore tree	shivela	(she-veigh-la)
white oak tree	tovashal	(toe-va-shawl)

SAY IT

abalone (ab-uh-LOH-nee) Abalone is a shellfish that can be eaten as food. Its shell has a hard, white lining called mother-of-pearl. Some Native Californians eat abalone and use the shell to make jewelry.

fluent (FLOO-uhnt) Someone who is fluent is able to speak a language easily and well. It takes a long time for someone to become fluent in a new language.

missions (MISH-uhnz) Missions are places that were established in California in the late 1700s and early 1800s to spread the Christian religion. Many California Native People were forced to live in missions.

oral histories (AWR-uhl HIS-tuh-rees) Oral histories are the history and memories of a people told out loud. Some oral histories tell how Native Peoples came to live on their lands.

powwow (POU-wouw) A powwow is a social gathering of Native Americans that usually includes dancing. Many Native Nations have powwows to celebrate their culture and traditions.

rancherias (ran-chah-REE-yas) Rancherias are another term for reservations. Reservations are called rancherias in some parts of California.

regalia (re-GAL-ee-a) Regalia are special clothes and decorations worn and used in ceremonies. Traditional regalia is part of many Native Nations' religious ceremonies.

reservations (rez-er-VAY-shuhns) Reservations are areas of land set aside for Native use. Reservations are run by their own governments and provide services to their residents.

sovereign (SAHV-ruhn) Something that is sovereign is independent. Native Nations recognized by the government are sovereign and can control their own affairs.

BOOKS

Aloian, Molly, and Bobbie Kalman. *Life of the California Coast Nations*. New York: Crabtree Publishing, 2004.

Feinstein, Stephen. *California Native Peoples*. 2nd ed. Chicago: Heinemann, 2009.

Marsh, Carole. *California Native Americans*. Peachtree City, GA: Gallopade International, 2004.

WEB SITES

Visit our Web site for links about Native Nations of California:

childsworld.com/links

Note to Parents, Teachers, and Librarians: We routinely verify our Web links to make sure they are safe and active sites. So encourage your readers to check them out!

TO LEARN MORE